The Oak Inside the Acorn

Max Lucado

Illustrations by George Angelini

A Division of Thomas Nelson Publishers
Since 1798

www.thomasnelson.com

To Steve and Becky Bryant,

with gratitude for your

countless acts of selfless service.

THE OAK INSIDE THE ACORN

Text and illustrations copyright © 2006 by Max Lucado.

Illustrations by George Angelini.

All rights reserved. No portion of this book may be reproduced in any form without the written permission of the publisher, with the exception of brief excerpts in reviews.

Published in Nashville, Tennessee, by Tommy Nelson®, a Division of Thomas Nelson®, Inc.

Visit us on the Web at www.tommynelson.com.

Tommy Nelson® books may be purchased in bulk for educational, business, fund-raising, or sales promotional use. For information, please email SpecialMarkets@ThomasNelson.com.

Library of Congress Cataloging-in-Publication Data

Lucado, Max.

    The oak inside the acorn / by Max Lucado ; illustrations by George Angelini.

       p. cm.

    Summary: A tiny acorn fulfills its destiny by becoming the tree God made it to be, and then it watches the little girl who climbs its branches grow up as well.

     ISBN-13: 978-1-4003-0601-5 (hardback)

     ISBN-10: 1-4003-0601-9

     [1. Growth—Fiction. 2. Acorns—Fiction. 3. Oak—Fiction. 4. Christian life—Fiction.]

I. Angelini, George, 1951–ill. II. Title.

PZ7.L9684Oa 2006

[E]—dc22

                                    2005033942

Printed in China

06 07 08 09 10 MT 5 4 3

Dear Parent,

God prewired your infant. He scripted your toddler's strengths. He set your teen on a trajectory. God gave you an eighteen-year research project. Ask yourself, your spouse, and your friends: What sets this child apart? Childhood tendencies forecast adult abilities. Read them. Discern them. Affirm them. Cheerlead them.

You've been given a book with no title—read it! A CD with no cover—listen to it! An island with no owner—explore it! Resist the urge to label before you study. Attend carefully to the unique childhood of your child.

Uncommon are the parents who attempt to learn these God-given abilities—and blessed are their children.

Blessings,
Max Lucado

The acorn looked at the world around him. Green hills rolled their backs in the distance. Bright daisies bloomed below him. Above him, a family of puffy white clouds floated through the blue sky.

"The world looks so big," the little acorn said to his mother. "I'm just glad to be right here with you."

His mother was a tall, beautiful oak tree. "I'm glad, too, my little acorn. It's good for you to be here with me now. But when your time comes to go into the world, you'll be fine."

"I'll be afraid."

Mother Oak hugged Little Acorn in her strong branches. "Within you is a great oak, Little Acorn. Just be the tree God made you to be."

The thought of letting go and leaving the safety of his mother's branches was scary to Little Acorn. So he tried not to think about it. But deep down inside, he knew the time was coming. One by one, his brothers and sisters had been letting go and saying good-bye. They had been afraid, too. But their mother had assured them with the same words: "Within you is a great oak. Just be the tree God made you to be."

Each time he heard this, Little Acorn would look at himself and say, "An oak, in me?" He was so small, it was hard for him to believe he could ever be a tree.

The time to let go came sooner than Little Acorn wanted. It started with a bump. He was resting one summer afternoon, thankful for the coolness in the shadow of the leaves, when—thud—the tree shook.

His mother's branches trembled, and Little Acorn began to swing back and forth. A farmer's pickup had accidentally backed into the tree trunk.

Little Acorn had swung before, stirred by the wind, bumped by climbing kids. And each time he'd always held on. But not this time. He tried. He pressed his thin stem into the branch as hard as he could. It didn't work. He was a heavier acorn than he used to be, and his stem began to pull away from the branch.

"Uh-oh . . . Mom?"

"It's okay, Little Acorn," Mother Oak assured him. "You can't hang on forever. It's time—you've got to let go."

Down he fell, flipping over and over, softly slipping through the leaves until he bounced on something hard. He had landed in the back of the pickup truck. The truck vibrated and began to drive away.

"It's okay, Little Acorn," his mom called out. "Within you is a great oak. Just be the tree God made you to be."

Little Acorn barely heard the last few words. The truck was already moving down the road. Going somewhere. He just didn't know where.

As the truck bounced, so did the acorn. "Ouch!" he said. "This is rough."

"It gets better," he heard a voice say. Rolling over, Little Acorn looked up at a young tree.

"Who are you?" he asked.

"I'm a new little orange tree on my way to be planted."

"What do orange trees do?" asked the acorn. (By now the road and the ride were smoother.)

"We grow oranges."

"Oh," answered the acorn. He didn't know what an orange was and was just about to ask when the truck slowed to a stop.

"Wow!" exclaimed Orange Tree, who was tall enough to see out of the truck.

"What is it?" asked the acorn.

"Trees. Orange trees. Everywhere. It's an orange grove."

"Okay, Little Orange Tree, it's time for you to be planted," the farmer said as he lowered the truck tailgate and climbed into the back of the truck.

The acorn rolled away just in time to avoid the farmer's big boot. The farmer took the tree and was gone for a long time. Little Acorn stared at the sky as it began to darken. He missed his mother oak and her strong branches. This would be his first night away from her.

The tailgate banged and the farmer jumped in. "A quick sweep," he said, "and I'm headed home." Little Acorn had never seen a broom. He barely saw this one before it sent him high in the air. He landed in soft dirt.

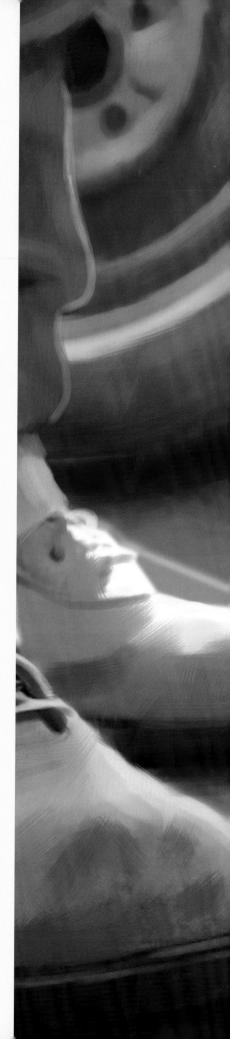

"I wondered what happened to you." It was Orange Tree.

Little Acorn was happy to hear a familiar voice. "Is this your new home?"

"It sure is," Orange Tree said. "And it looks like it's your home, too."

Little Acorn had one more question. "Orange Tree, what do I do next?"

Orange Tree's voice was sleepy. "Just settle in, little friend, and rest. God will make you grow."

And so Little Acorn did just that. He rested. That night. The next day. That week. The next month. There in the soft soil surrounded by orange trees, he sank deeper and deeper into the ground and slumbered. He slept a long, long time.

When Little Acorn awoke, he didn't know where he was. He stretched upward, and when he did, he kept stretching higher and higher until he popped out of the dark dirt into the sunlight.

"Well, look who's awake," announced Orange Tree. Little Acorn looked around and then up.

"Hello, Orange Tree. Have I been sleeping long?"

"Long enough to become a small tree."

Little Acorn looked down at himself and said, "I've changed." His round shell was now a slender trunk.

"You are growing up," Orange Tree said. "Now you are a little oak."

Little Oak straightened himself and remembered his mother's words: "Within you is a great oak. . . ." *Maybe she was right,* he thought, and he stood a bit taller.

But even at his tallest, he was much smaller than the big orange trees. Their bushy branches grew greener and greener. Then, one day, Orange Tree called out to his friend, "Little Oak, look! My first orange."

The big orange trees spoke up. "He'll have many more," they said.

"So will I!" announced Little Oak. The trees in the grove laughed. They didn't mean to hurt Little Oak's feelings . . . but they did.

"You'll never have oranges," they said, chuckling.

Little Oak straightened his branches and pushed as hard as he could, but no oranges popped out. Not that day. Nor the next. Nor the next.

When the farmer came to collect the fruit, Little Oak was worried—he had none to give.

"Well, hello, Little Oak," the farmer greeted. "How did you get here?"

The farmer walked away, and when he returned, he carried a big shovel.

"I know just the place for you."

He lifted the new little oak tree out of the ground.

"Bye-bye, my friend," said Orange Tree.

The farmer didn't take Little Oak too far away. He carried him out of the grove to his big white house. The farmer chose a spot in the backyard, overlooking the orange grove. "Let's see how you do here," he said. Then he dug a deep hole and set Little Oak inside it. He placed dirt around Little Oak and pressed it tightly around the tree's roots.

Little Oak liked his new home. For the first time, he stood taller than almost everything around him.

Little Oak was stretching his roots into the dirt when he heard, "Hi, I'm Pink Petunia. Who are you?" Little Oak looked at the bright flower near the house. He started to answer, but Pink Petunia didn't give him time. "Rosie is next to the house."

"Hi there," chirped Rosie.

"Daisy is here, too."

"That's me," said a white and yellow flower. "Hello, little tree."

Pink Petunia continued, "We are soft and smell sweet. What about you?"

Little Oak didn't know how to answer. He knew he had no oranges.

"Do you grow flowers?" Pink Petunia asked.

Little Oak never remembered seeing flowers like roses or petunias on his mother. But still, maybe oaks did grow flowers. "Maybe I could. Maybe that is what I'm made to do," he answered.

So he tried. As hard as he could, Little Oak tried to grow flowers like his friends could grow. As the sun grew hotter, they unfolded into a rainbow of pinks, reds, and yellows. Little Oak, however, just grew taller. As the days grew longer, his roots grew deeper. Every day, he tried to grow colorful flowers. But he never could.

Pink Petunia could. So could Rosie. So could Daisy. But not Little Oak.

Finally Little Oak decided to rest. His branches were tired and drooping. His leaves were dropping. Even the flowers were sleepy.

"We're going to rest now, Little Oak," the flowers told him. And they did. The sky grayed and days shortened and the whole garden slept. While Little Oak slept, he dreamed. He dreamed of his days as a little acorn on his mother's branch. Deep in his sleep, he heard her soft voice: "Within you is a great oak. Just be the tree God made you to be."

When the sun warmed his branches, Little Oak awoke. Only he wasn't so little anymore. He could see farther. He had grown taller. And wider. The winds didn't bend him as much. His branches were as big as his trunk used to be. Little Oak was becoming Big Oak.

Many years passed, and each
year he grew bigger and wider,
wider and bigger, until everything
in the farmer's yard looked up to him.

Now Orange Tree and the flowers called him Big Oak. He spread his big branches and looked around. Orange Tree was taller, too. But not as tall as Big Oak. Big Oak was taller than all his friends. They were wide, but not as wide as Big Oak. He was the tallest. He was the widest. But he still wondered what he was supposed to do. He couldn't grow oranges or flowers. He just grew bigger. And he didn't know why.

Big Oak was just awakening from a long winter's nap, his leaves tiny buds, when a young farmer brought two ropes and tied them to one of his strong branches. Close by, a little girl watched.

Rosie Rose was puzzled. "What's it for, Big Oak?"

"I don't know," Big Oak answered. But he soon found out.

"Can I do it, Daddy? Can I swing?"

"Go ahead," urged the man, and the little girl with bright blue eyes and hair the color of Daisy's flowers sat in the swing. Big Oak felt the tug, but barely. He was strong and Little Girl was small. With her daddy's help, she swung forward. Not too far. But farther the next day and farther the next . . .

By the time the sun was hot and the flowers were plenty, she could swing alone—kicking her feet higher and higher until she could see the roof of her house. Then back she would swing—back until she seemed to look straight at the ground.

Big Oak loved the sound of Little Girl's laughter, her footsteps running toward him, her squeals of delight as she swung higher and higher into the sky. Yes, Big Oak loved Little Girl.

When she swung, he stood strong. When her daddy built her a tree house in Big Oak's branches, Big Oak gladly held it. When Little Girl stretched out on the grass to watch the clouds float, Big Oak shaded her. She played in his branches, climbed his trunk, rested in his shadow, and together they grew.

Each year both taller.

Each year both stronger.

When gray skies brought cold days, Big Oak slept and the swing hung silent and the playhouse stayed empty. When blue skies brought warm days, they laughed and played. Little Girl talked, and he listened. And at last Big Oak knew he had become the tree God made him to be.

One day Little Girl came to Big Oak with
a little boy—though neither was too little.
They sat on his branches and talked. Big
Oak held them both. And when they
carved their names on his trunk, he didn't
mind.

Little Boy pushed the swing. Little Girl
laughed, and Big Oak protected them
from the sudden rain.

In time, Little Girl didn't swing so much.
When she climbed into the tree house,
she sat more and played less. Little Girl
was becoming Big Girl.

Big Girl now stood as tall as Big Oak's lowest branch.

One day Rosie Rose said to Big Oak, "She's growing up, Big Oak. She'll soon leave."

Big Oak didn't answer, but he understood.

Big Girl spent many blue-sky days sitting on the ground, leaning back against Big Oak's trunk and watching the clouds drift by. Big Oak knew Big Girl had a big question on her mind, because she said things like:

"I don't know what I'm supposed to be."

And: "It's hard to let go."

And: "How can I know who I am?"

Big Oak wanted to talk to Big Girl. He knew just what to say. He would say, "Within you is a great girl. Just be the person God made you to be.

"Orange trees grow oranges," he would say. "Flower plants grow flowers. And oaks? Oaks grow tall enough for swings and strong enough for swinging and big enough to hold little girls until they become big girls."

He wanted to. But he couldn't say the words.

One day Big Girl was so sad. The little girl who used to giggle in Big Oak's shade just sat, silent tears flowing down her cheeks.

"It's hard to let go," she said.

Big Oak was listening, and he had an idea. He looked down his branch at a little acorn. "I have a special job for you," Big Oak said.

The next time the wind blew his branches, Big Oak let this branch shake more than the others. The little acorn popped loose and landed in Big Girl's lap.

Big Girl picked it up and started to toss it away but stopped. She held the little acorn in her hand and stared at it. She turned and looked up at Big Oak. "Were you ever this small?" Answering her own question she continued, "Of course you were. You grew into a great oak from a little acorn. All you did was become what God made you to be."

She looked again at the acorn, then back at the tree. Her eyes brightened. "Do you suppose that's what God wants me to do?"

Big Oak wanted to shout, "Yes!" But he didn't have to. Big Girl stood and announced, "Of course He does. Now, it's time for me to let go and become the person God made me to be."

Big Girl smiled, placed the acorn in her pocket,
and began walking away. But after a few steps, she
stopped and turned. She looked at the swing.
The tree house. She looked at Big Oak. She
walked over to him and placed a hand
on his trunk.

Without a word,
she said good-bye.

Without a word,
Big Oak said
the same.